A Treasure Chest of Best-Loved Poems

J.H. Lockhart

Copyright © 2019 by J.H. Lockhart.

ISBN   Softcover   978-1-950580-52-1

All rights reserved. No part of this book may be reproduced or transmitted in any form or by any means, electronic or mechanical, including photocopying, recording, or by any information storage and retrieval system without express written permission from the author, except in the case of brief quotations embodied in critical reviews and certain other non-commercial uses permitted by copyright law.

Printed in the United States of America.

To order additional copies of this book, contact:
Bookwhip
1-855-339-3589
https://www.bookwhip.com

Dedication

In writing this Dedication, I am cognizant of the words found in the Holy Bible, Romans 12:12, which says, *"Be joyful in hope, patient in affliction, faithful in prayer."*

These words bring to mind three extraordinary women who have had the most superlative impact on my life -- through their expressions of hope for my success in life; patience in the face of my impatience, despite whatever afflictions each faced (of one type or another); faithfulness; and a sincere belief in the power of prayer.

I am talking about my blessed Mom, the late Connie Lockhart Gordon; the late Esther Mae Murphy Lockhart, mother of my beautiful daughters, Angela Fisher and Lisa Lockhart McCoy; and my wife, Dr. Maria Carrington Lockhart, a brilliant, internationally-known educator and inspirational leader.

Many of my most honored works that have been labeled "Delightful" by poetry lovers were inspired by these wonderful ladies.

Introduction

Welcome! This book has been compiled especially for YOU, as one who is seeking a volume of inspiration in the areas of Faith, Love, and Humor ("Fun").

Now, please be aware that this collection of some of my most-loved, award-winning and "delightful" works is intended for you, who will be motivated to "go back to the well" OFTEN in pursuit of the reaffirmation of your faith in the Lord, to find passages to express your love for your "significant other," and/or to just find the words that elicit a smile or a hearty laugh.

                    ENJOY!

Preface

It has been gratifying to hear and read the multiple compliments and accolades for the poetic works of this, your humble servant.

However, the purpose of the Preface is not to boast or echo the much-appreciated accolades for my work, but to thank the Good Lord, the proponents of my work, and those who will be introduced to these "delights" for the first time. Incidentally, the term "delightful," in reference to my past works, stems not from my own assessment of my works, which would reflect blatant egotism, but from the actual use of the term as expressed by a number of people who have heard and read my works.

I would be remiss if I did not thank Darchelle M. Garner, who assisted with editing this book. It is a continuous joy to write a major poetic component for the popular monthly newsletter, of which Ms. Garner is Editor, of The People's Community Baptist Church (TPCBC) in Silver Spring, Maryland, where Dr. Haywood A. Robinson, III, serves as Pastor. I am also grateful to Rochelle Sumner, TPCBC's Communications Director, for designing the cover of this book.

The poems in *A Treasure Chest of the Best-Loved Poems of J.H. Lockhart"* are presented in three categories: **Faith, Love** and **Funny Stuff**.

The *Faith* section includes such works as, "I Have Seen Miracles," which puts forth these points:

> *Oh, yes, I have seen miracles, every day, haven't you?*
> *Despite the evil that some men do*

The *Love* component the poem awarded a Gold Medal by The National Society of Poets, "My Mother's Prayer," excerpted here:

> *I know good and well that I am only here*
> *As the result of the power of my mother's prayer.*

And in the *Funny Stuff* section, you will find such humorous works as "Don't Go Shopping with Her." Here's a taste:

> *Hope you have found "the love of your life"*
> *And are looking forward to the day she becomes your lawfully wedded wife!*
> *But, permit me, your older brother, to give you a word of advice:*
> *Don't go shopping with her!*

Read on and enjoy, Dear Reader.

Table of Contents

FAITH

My Mother's Prayer	3
Delightful!	5
Getting to Know You	7
He's Watching You and Me!	9
Mothers: God's Special Blessing to Us All	11
In Praise of *Dads*; Concerns about *Fathers*	13
Today's Dream	15
The Day I Met the Rev. Martin Luther King, Jr.	17
Never Stop Pursuing that Goal!	19
The Prayer of Parents	21
Don't Let Your Dream Fade Away	23
The Machinations of Satan	25
Introspection	27
Let's Define "Good News"	29
Don't Let the Economy Get You Down!	31
A Fervent Prayer	33
I Have Seen Miracles	35
A Message for All: Are You Ready for Fall?	37
Christmas is Here for You!	39
Reflections on Faith	41
An Easter Prayer -- From the Heart	43
Don't Wait Until Thanksgiving!	45
Some Happy Thanksgiving Thoughts	47
Let It Shine!	49

LOVE

My Love for You 53
To Maria with Sincere Love 55
Dedicated to My Wonderful Wife: Dr. Maria Carrington Lockhart. . . . 57
To My Beautiful Wife, Maria, on Mother's Day 2017 59
A Loving Happy Valentine's Day to Maria 61
What a Friend We Have in Mothers! 63
The Best Gift of Christmas. 65
What I Really Need for Christmas 67

FUNNY STUFF

Don't Go Shopping With Her! 71
A Funny Story: My Uncle's Rebounding Hat 73
How I Got Over: That Ol' Bully 75
My Hilarious Buddy -- Little Willie Smith 77
Shopping: The Difference Between Women and Men 79
The Racist I Met One Day 81
Sometimes You Have to Laugh 83
Little Delights! 85

FAITH

My Mother's Prayer

I know good and well that I am only here
As the result of the power of my mother's prayer.
Everything I am and everything I'll ever be
Has come through the grace of God
And my mother's prayers for me!
From the moment of my conception
Through the nine months she carried me,
I somehow knew, even then,
That my mother was praying for me.
As a child growing up with a tendency
To be as precocious as I could possibly be,
I still learned the importance of moral values
Listening to my mother's prayers for me.
And now, since I am grown -- an official adult,
It's comforting to know that even from Heaven,
Even from up there,
My mother takes time from her angelic duties
To remember me in her daily prayer!

Delightful!

What makes you feel delightful?
I believe it's feeling true love in your heart.
What makes a person delightful?
I believe it's reflecting faith and being "smart,"

Smart enough to have a positive sense of self
Smart enough to look out for others besides
Yourself.
The most delightful persons are unselfish and kind.
The most delightful person I ever met was the loving
Mother of mine.

We can delight in many things in life.
With faith, we can find delight, despite economic or
Other strife.
Even when you feel despair, you can find delight
Upon remembering that God is here and everywhere.

As a creative writer, a poet who seeks to be loving,
Not spiteful,
It is a blessing, a joy to write works like this
That folks can read and find delightful!

Getting to Know You

I fondly remember the musical, *The King and I*, don't you?
I was particularly touched by the song
Entitled, "Getting to Know You."

Remember? It goes something like this:

"Getting to know you,
Getting to know all about you.
Getting to like you,
Getting to know what you say…
Because of all the beautiful and new things
I am learning about you, day by day."

Now, that's what I believe
You and I should do,
So that in the future,
We don't make one another blue.

If we take the time to get to know
One another's dreams, hopes,
Wishes and desires,
We would have already taken steps
To put out any interpersonal fires.

This way, we would have a chance to see
If this strong initial attraction
Really is for real,
And likely avoid any misunderstanding
That could get in our way,

And help lead us to what I believe
Will be many a beautiful day.

He's Watching You and Me!

You can "put on airs."
You can "play it cool,"
And thus take the general public
And friends & family "for the fool!"
You can "dress to the nines."
You can smile your most awesome smile,
But there is one thing that's for sure:
The Good Lord is watching you
Every moment, all the while!
Let us never forget
That God sees and knows
The real, the authentic you and me.
Don't you see that the Eyes of the Lord
Are focused and will always be?
Amen!

Mothers: God's Special Blessing to Us All

I've said it before and I'll say it again:
Mothers were sent by God as our special blessing!
From Mary, chosen to be the mother of Jesus on earth,
To that very special mother chosen by Him to give you birth --
Mothers like mine, so imbued with love and compassion.
Mothers in my life -- with the title of wife,
Who, although modern and fashionable,
When it came to "mother wit"
Demonstrated as mothers
At times it was important to be "old fashioned,"
"old fashioned" in the sense that mothers
Were created to be,
As teachers, counselors, helping us, their children,
To become the best we can be.
God bless each of you who holds the title "mother."
You are truly His special blessing.
And we, your and His children,
Just want you to know we sure love ya!

In Praise of Dads; Concerns about Fathers

Hope the title of this piece caught your eye
And made you wonder what "Doc" Lockhart is trying to say!
The point is: Let us give our love and praise to men who take seriously
Their role as *Dad*!
At the same time, men who are merely *fathers*
Make me feel sad!
Dads are men who fully demonstrate their joy
In loving and supporting their child,
While mere *fathers* are men who participate in the child-conception process,
But then walk away, or stay away,
To leave the mother to the child-rearing process.
So, let us pray our most ardent prayer to the Good Lord,
The Loving Father of us all,
That the day will come that a mere *father*
Becomes a *Dad*,
And the mother of his child and the child
Will have reasons to rejoice and be glad.

Today's Dream

As Our Children Begin the School Year
(What I believe Dr. Martin Luther King, Jr., would say about recent events)

I have a dream
That the tragedies of Michael Brown, Trayvon Martin, and other victims
of atrocious and hateful gun violence
Will lead to the positive changes
This nation must attain.

I have a dream
That such atrocities will cease
Throughout America
And never, and I mean <u>never</u>,
<u>Ever</u>, happen again!

I have a dream
That parents from all ethnic, cultural and linguistic backgrounds
will join forces
To help ALL CHILDREN make a resounding difference.

I have a dream
That a cross-section of African-American kids,
Caucasian kids, Hispanic kids,
Asian kids, (WHATEVER BACKGROUND THE KIDS)
will bridge the cultural and linguistic gaps
In recognition that there is potential in all kids
To be bright and beautiful "whiz" kids.

I have a dream that no parent, like no child,
Will be left behind in pursuit of upward mobility,
And that soon and very soon
Students from every community in the U.S.
Will succeed academically, socially
And economically.

The Day I Met the Rev. Martin Luther King, Jr.

The day I met Martin Luther King
Is a day I keep remembering.
It was August 28, 1963,
And nine busloads of multi-ethnic folks
Were willing to follow me!
We had traveled from upstate N.Y. cities
Of Albany, Troy and Schenectady
To join the 1963 March On Washington,
And each one of us was determined
And each of us was ready!
Four hundred and fifty strong
Of men and woman – black, white & brown
And we were not going to let any opponent of civil rights
Do or say anything to turn us around!
We left the Albany area at midnight
On August 27, nineteen and sixty three,
And traveled all night long
While I kept wondering why these good folks
Had up and chosen me.
I was basically "a kid" barely out of college,
And while I had demonstrated some courage and leadership,
I knew I had not solely been the one to win past civil rights battles
That my dad and Alpha Phi Alpha founder, George Biddle Kelley, had won.
I had been selected because I was, respectively, their son and godson.
When we arrived in D.C., early in the morning,
Every delegation leader was summoned to a meeting of encouragement
and warning.
We were directed to the base of the Lincoln memorial for a brief meeting
And an opportunity to shake hands with the March planners
and other great leaders.

What a joy it was to meet A. Philip Randolph, Andrew Young,
and others worth remembering!
But I was most impressed with the serenity and dignity
of Martin Luther King.
He shook my hand and I noticed that his eyes had a beam.
Little did I know that momentarily he would shortly thereafter electrify
the world
With his magnificent speech referred to as
"I Have a Dream…"
As the years have passed, and I have fond memories worth remembering,
I shall never forget that wonderful day when I was blessed to meet
The exceptional man of grace, dignity, and yet humility --
The one and only Martin Luther King, Jr. What a lasting inspiration to
you and to me!

Never Stop Pursuing that Goal!

Lately I've met so many folks
who have given up on what were their "life-long" goals.
Folks who are not necessarily "old folks,"
But who now believe that their childhood dreams
Are tantamount to self-deceptive "jokes."
No, I'm not talking about that outrageous dream
Where the pursuit of the goal
May have been way too extreme,
Like my "kid-friend" who said he was going to move to the moon
And who said he wasn't going to wait until he got old.
He was going to go on up there "real soon!"
In retrospect, I should have apologized to him,
Because I was one of the crowd who called him "looney."
But even "looney," now a successful musician,
Had a right to his dream.
And who knows how "high" he could have gone
If we had not made fun of him.
But I'm talking about setting goals that you begin to think
are just out of reach
And just seem to fade away even with your plan.
And other opportunities come along -- so there!
So you just give up and forget the tale of the little ol' train
Who achieved his goal because he kept telling himself,
"I think I can."

The Prayer of Parents

O Lord, Omnipotent Father, we give
You thanks for having given us
Children.

Thank You for giving us Your only
Begotten Son, our anointed Lord
And Savior, Jesus, in whose Name we
Pray this morning.

You have given us the awesome
Responsibility to love, nurture, and
Raise our children in accordance with Thy Word.

Our children and our joy, and we
Accept, with serenity, the worries,
Fears, and labors that are integral
To our role as parents.

Help us to nourish them with
Sincere love and guidance.

Through us You gave life to
Them…Through eternity You knew
Them and loved them.

Don't Let Your Dream Fade Away

Yes, you are getting older every day,
And it seems that your special dream is fading away.
And with each passing day and night
You feel your special dream has gone out of sight.
But that does not have to be your fate,
Because there are many successful folks
Whose dreams of success came "kinda late."
With faith in God and confidence in you,
Age "ain't nothin' but a number"
And age need not prevent you from doing
What you always wanted to do.
Give you some examples, from more recent days.
Sure, although our biblical lessons about
such folks as Abraham and Sarah will never fade away,
How about Nelson Mandela
when he was 74 years "young."
And, space permitting, I could name many, many more,
Like Ray Kroc, who founded a business you have all supported called
McDonald's
when he was around 55, or more.
Oh, your humble servant could write on this theme "for days,"
but the point is: don't you, dear reader,
let your ambition be determined by your age.

The Machinations of Satan

You are not paranoid to feel that Satan's out to get you.
His constant machinations (schemes) are evil tricks to trap you.
For instance, it may be really inviting to see something that does not belong to you,
While Satan is whispering in your ear
"Go ahead and do what you want to do."
And if he succeeds in tempting you,
he just laughs that he has up and tempted another "fool."
Oh, you are saying, "I'm too strong
and have too much Christian strength to fall under Satan's spell.
And besides I'm planning to go to Heaven and not down to Satan's hell."
Well, permit me to share with you, strong one,
That, far too often, Satan and his minions have won.
The history of the world is oh so replete with the evil that Satan and his ilk have done.
We don't even have to go back to the snake who tempted Eve
Or all the "devils" throughout the years who had evil up their sleeve.
Just look around today's world, our country, your neighborhood.
Now, I won't mention any names, but you know full well that I could.
Now, that's not to say we should look at the speck in someone else's eye,
while ignoring the log in our own.
But being aware of temptations
and being faithful to "the Good Lord"
is the purpose and point of this poem.

Introspection

Do you engage in periodic introspection?
No, it's not something naughty;
It's the practice of self-inspection.
Every now and then we need to take a look
Inside,
With an honest assessment and without false
Pride.
Ask yourself, "Am I all that I need
To be?
Am I letting the Holy Spirit speak wisdom
To me?"
Ask, "Do I have compassion for those
In need?
Do I practice self-control to eschew that
Evil deed?"
Introspection is a means to cleanse the
Heart and soul,
And is of major value to everyone, be ye
Young or old!
Try it, and you will see that introspection is
Worth the while.
Although some folks start out frowning
At themselves,
Most folks end up their introspection
With a smile!

Let's Define "Good News"

The stuff you read in the paper
Is usually anything but "good news."
As a matter of fact,
Most of the newspaper fare
Does nothin' but give you "the blues,"
With their practice of "If it bleeds it leads."
Newspapers tend to feature the worst
Features of life, such as
Disasters, tragedies, and economic strife.
And the broadcast media does exactly the same
With its obsession with scandal and turmoil
And the political "game."
So, if you are looking for "good news,"
Turn to the words of our Lord
With the Good News of our Savior
And the wisdom of **His Word**.
Now, that's the Good News
That will do your heart some good
And enhance your soul with joy,
And will strengthen you
As *good news* should.

Don't Let the Economy Get You Down!

These days, I see so many folks
Wearing a frown.
A major reason is 'cause today's economy
Has made them feel so down.

With job losses, foreclosures,
And such other bad news,
One finds even former faithful Christians
Are beset with frustration and "the blues."

Don't let this frustration
Happen to you.
Listen, my brother, my sister.
Here's what you need to do:

First, remember God's promise
When He said, "I will not forsake you."
Also remember when Jesus said
"I am always with you."

You and I must get our faith in Him
Back in our hearts and minds.
No, nobody said that having faith is easy,
But rekindling your faith is certainly stronger…

Why? Because history is replete
With examples of God rewarding faith.
He has proven time and time again that
He will reach out to you if you reach out to Him in
Faith.

I know that He has shown this fact to me
Whenever I resisted losing faith in Him.
I also know that He will come through for you.
Try it. Go to Him in prayer, and watch what He will do.

A Fervent Prayer

Listen to my voice in the morning, Lord. (Psalm 5:3a)

Brothers and sisters in Christ, as we focus our hearts and minds on God, the Father, God the Son Jesus, and God the Holy Spirit, let us pray for our individual needs as well as corporately for the many troubles of the world today.

Let us pray, grateful that we have been granted, each of us, the grace and mercy to be able to lift up our Lord and Savior -- as we lift up those, like ourselves, in need of prayer.

Dear Lord, we come to You reflecting both humility and strength, humble in acknowledging Your awesome capacity to love us, guide us, and protect us despite our human frailties in the areas of thought, words and deeds.

Today, when we are constantly confronted with the news of the trials and tribulations of our nation, such as the devastating flooding in Texas and the surrounding areas, the troubles with ruthless dictators and heartless assassins and those would-be rulers who are so self-centered that they do harm every day in one manner or another, we pray for Your mercy, guidance and protection. Guide us, Heavenly Father, and help us to understand and take individual action, acceptable in Your sight, regarding the Black Lives Matter movement, as You guided and protected us through the precursor of this movement, the Civil Rights Movement.

Thank You, Lord, for permitting us to live to see the awesome National Museum of African-American History and Culture, which so vividly depicts the oppression, struggles and achievements of our people throughout the history of this nation.

Help us to pray fervently that You bless and uplift each and every one who is sick, shut-in, anxious, bereaved, or in need of financial blessing. And, as we live every day in this troubled world, let us not let the troubles of the world dampen our faith and the knowledge that You are always here to take our hand, Precious Lord.

We pray this prayer in Jesus' Name.

Amen.

I Have Seen Miracles

What an awesome, marvelous God we serve,
Who provides blessings and spiritual guidance
Sometimes beyond that which I believe that I deserve,
Who always is there to receive a fervent prayer
With the blessed assurance that He is everywhere!
Oh, sometimes, like a heathen, I guess,
I have wondered if my prayer request even reaches Him,
When, all of a sudden, I hear in my ears
And heart a memorable sermon
Or my favorite hymn.
And, looking around me, my eyes reveal
That all that is good and righteous
Is a most vivid reflection of Him.
Oh, yes, I have seen miracles, every day, haven't you?
Despite the evil that some men do,
I find it imperative that I look through Christian eyes
And realize that God's everlasting grace and mercy
Should come as no surprise.

A Message for All: Are You Ready for Fall?

Brother, Sister, Youth-in-Christ:
Are you ready for the Fall?
No, I'm not talking about falling down,
Nor falling in love,
Nor falling for the trick of some "clown."
I'm asking if you are ready for the season known as "Fall."
I'm asking if you are ready for "The Avalanche,"
The myriad temptations
That come at you and me every Fall?
Whether you are an elementary school student
Determined to achieve!
Whether you are a secondary school student
Ready to defeat the many negative challenges
That you are bound to meet!
Whether you are a college student
Facing the myriad demands
That it takes if you are to succeed!
Whether you are an adult
With the stress and strains of work, family
And the multitude of demands you find yourself facing daily!
Whether you are a "Senior Citizen," a member of "Generation One,"
Who has faced many challenges -- some you have lost,
Some you have won!
The question we must ALL ask ourselves is
Am I spiritually, morally and emotionally prepared?
With the blessed assurance
that the good Lord is with me,
I have absolutely no reason to be scared!

Christmas is Here for You!

Dear Brothers and Sisters,
Whatever you do,
Take the time to acknowledge that Christmas is for you.
Regardless of your circumstances
Or that "trial" that you are going through,
Remember that Jesus came to Earth
To bless and protect
Both me and you!
With all the shopping and partying
That folks are going through,
None of that carries the true message
That Jesus was born to bless you!

During this blessed holiday season
Some folks tend to forget
"The reason for the season,"
That "Christmas" stands for "Christ's Mass,"
And that celebration of His Birth
Is the first and foremost reason for this season.

Oh, yes, Santa Claus and Frosty
And all that so-called holiday stuff
May be their major focus,
But God knows
That "stuff" is not enough.

Oh, there is little wrong, I guess,
With celebrating in their own way,
But Santa Claus, Frosty, and Rudolph
Certainly aren't going to save us
When we meet the Lord
On Judgment Day.

So, Brothers and Sisters and Young Folks, too,
Take time to acknowledge
That Christ was born for you.

Reflections on Faith

Let us reflect upon and draw some poetic thoughts from this and other Scripture:
Hebrews 11:1-4, from the Faith Chapter

1. *Faith is being sure of what we hope for and certain of what we do not see…*
   That is the perfect focus for Christians, like you and me!

2. *By faith we understand that the universe was formed at God's command…*
   How blessed we are that he let us mere mortals dwell upon his land!

3. *By faith Abel offered God a better sacrifice than Cain did…*
   Through faith we know He has forgiven us for past sins we committed.

4. Psalm 46:1: *God is our refuge and strength, an ever present help in trouble.*
   He makes our good fortune double.

5. John 8:12: *Jesus said, I am the light of the world, whoever follows me will never walk in darkness, but will have the light of life.*
   The Savior thus pointed out that He will rescue us from the strafes of life.

6. Romans 12:12: *Be joyful in hope, patient in affliction, faithful in prayer.*
   Know in your heart that through faith and prayer God will be there.

7. Psalm 9:10: *Those who know your name will trust in you, for you, Lord, have never forsaken those who seek you.*
   How true! How gloriously true!

An Easter Prayer -- From the Heart

God is our refuge and strength, an ever-present help in trouble. (Psalm 46:1)

Although a multitude of days, years, and centuries have come to pass,
The miracle of Your resurrection, Dear Lord,
Is the blessed assurance
That will *always* last!

Thank You and bless You, Dear Brother Jesus,
and thanks be to God the Father Who sent You,
His only begotten Son, to redeem us through Your suffering on the Cross,
Enduring excruciating pain and agony
To atone for the sins of Your children, like me!
You rose from the dead
On that blessed Sunday morn
So that sinners, like me, could be forgiven through Thee.

Thank You, again, beloved Jesus,
For the miracle that allows us, Your loving Christians,
Through our prayers and worship,
To be saved as we strive to be sin-free!
Guide us and keep us on this and every day
And receive our prayer, Dear Jesus,
as in Your blessed Name we pray. Amen.

Don't Wait Until Thanksgiving!

I know some folks who only thank the Lord on Thanksgiving Day.
Now, I'm not trying to judge, nor trying to tell folks when and how to pray,
But if you will give me this chance
Here's what I would like to say…
I find great guidance in Psalm 107.
And I kind of believe the words of this Psalm
Will bring one closer to going to Heaven.
Just verse one of Psalm 107 makes the point I'm making understood.
It says, and I quote:
"Give thanks to the Lord, for he is good."
Do we, so often, take for granted the blessings that He gives us?
Do we feel that there's no need to pray 'cause everything is alright with us?
Now, I'm not "getting on your case,"
'cause I'm just as guilty, too.
But don't you agree that the admonition in these words
Gives one hundred percent guidance
To me and you?

Some Happy Thanksgiving Thoughts

Happy Thanksgiving: You and I have been blessed
To live here on earth for another year;
And despite the challenges all around us,
Our Lord and Savior has kept us on solid ground.
Despite any aches or pains
Loss of loved ones, or other issues that we face,
Let us praise Him for all of His mercy
And His loving, saving grace.

If through adversity you have trod,'
Yet, with a serene and smiling face
And believed more in His saving grace
Than hypocrisy and cranks,
For this let's give Him thanks.

If you have, somehow, worried less
Through the ups and downs
Along life's sometimes challenging track
And have remained undaunted and not looked back
And kept on smiling through Satan's pranks,
For this now raise your arms to Him
And shout out your word of "Thanks."

Let It Shine!

The Good Lord has granted a very special blessing
That is strictly yours and mine.
It is our own unique gift, our own special smile,
Our smile that God wants us to share without hesitation.
So let it shine!
Let it shine as an expression of the many blessings
He grants you every day.
Let it shine
To reflect that you won't let any negatives
Hamper your love for Him in any way.
Let it shine
So you will feel His blessings through the night.
Let it shine
So that smile on your face will light up your life,
Reminding you that He consistently blesses you from above.
Let it shine,
For, by letting it shine,
You will be both the giver and the recipient of love.

LOVE

My Love for You

I've been loving you a long time.
That's a fact, without doubt.
We have not always had a smooth time,
But, my heart never put you out.

Probably the hardest thing for you to
Believe
Is that I've always been faithful to you.
That fact is even hard for me to believe.
So, if you doubt me, I don't blame you.

Oh, there was that time when I got mad
And cheating entered my mind,
But, I realized that, once I did,
I could never again call you "mine."

Someday, I hope you will believe me,
And we can be closer in love and trust,
Because my love for you isn't a plaything.
My love for you is *a must*.

Sincerely,
Jim
Valentine's Day

To Maria with Sincere Love

Happy Birthday

A Message Written Especially for You

Maria, thank you for your love.
You know, it's easy to get caught up
In the little everyday stuff of life
And not tell you the big things that really matter.
That's why on your birthday,
I want to make sure that you know
That I am grateful for the woman you are
And the love you add to my life.
And even when I don't say it,
I'm glad to be sharing
Both the big days
And the every days
With you: my so very special wife.
Happy Birthday!

Dedicated to My Wonderful Wife: Dr. Maria Carrington Lockhart

Mother's Day 2016

It doesn't have to be "Mother's Day" to tell you that I love you.
It doesn't have to be "Mother's Day to show you that I care.
I feel blessed each and every day
Just to know you are here!
I may not always say it,
And sometimes we may disagree,
But regardless of whether we agree or disagree,
You still mean the world to me.
I truly appreciate all the loving things you do
And I can't imagine living in a world without you.
You have so much intelligence
Mixed with being good lookin' too.
Like I said, I really thank the Good Lord
For matching me up with you.
Let's endeavor to be loving and positive
On this and every day
And again, Happy Mother's Day,
Which I pray you will enjoy in every possible way.

To My Beautiful Wife, Maria, on Mother's Day 2017

Maria, when I look back
On all of our
Sweet moments,
Exciting times together,
Day to day tasks,
And wonderful accomplishments,
I can't imagine anyone
Who would have been
A better wife and love.
I realize just how blessed
I am by the Good Lord up above.
You make our life
Enjoyable and exciting each and every day.
And even if we may occasionally disagree,
I truly love you this Mother's Day
And every day!

A Loving Happy Valentine's Day to Maria

To my beautiful, amazing, talented, and loving wife,
Dr. Maria Carrington Lockhart, the love of my life.
Let me take this opportunity to say
My love for you is constant and will never go away.
Oh, I know that from time to time I get on your nerves
And practically "drive you up the wall,"
But, believe me, I don't mean any harm,
Because even then, I love you most of all.
You are such a hard worker
And dedicated to whatever you do
That sometimes I just plain worry about you,
Because of all the many, many things you do.
But I will always love you
And that's the bottom line.
And I thank the Good Lord every day, every night
That He has made you mine.

What a Friend We Have in Mothers!

What a friend we have in mothers,
All our aches and pains to bear.
Where would we be without our mothers?
I don't know about you,
But I would be nowhere!
Oh, how often we take for granted
The wonderful woman who gave us birth.
Sometimes we think that like a rose
She was just planted
On God's green earth!
We tend to forget that, through God's mercy,
Moms were placed upon this earth.
Whenever we feel weak or heavy-laden,
Burdened with "a world of care,"
Yes, we may turn to God for His mercy,
But he gave the nurturing assignment to Mother Dear.

The Best Gift of Christmas

The best gift of Christmas
Is easy to see.

It's not wrapped in paper
Or under the tree.

'Cause the best gift of Christmas and all the year through
Is having a spouse
As special as you.

What I Really Need for Christmas

Though you gave me more than I deserve for Christmas,
There is just one thing I really need.

Look me in the eyes,
And I'm sure that you will see
Love that shines so brightly,
Attraction that's super strong.

I love you so much, Honey.
You're my Christmas all year long.

FUNNY STUFF

Don't Go Shopping With Her!

(Advice to My Younger Brother)

Hope you have found "the love of your life"
And are looking forward to the day she becomes your lawfully wedded wife!
But, permit me, your older brother, to give you a word of advice:
Don't go shopping with her!
Now, I'm sure that she's exceptional, and, like my wife, a wonderful lady,
But, your brother here would just like to warn you,
So on the very first day you will be ready.
You see, shopping is a woman's most favorite thing,
Just like football, basketball, baseball or whatever may be your favorite thing.
So to most women, going shopping is tantamount to going to "the game."
So, this message is not to knock their manner of fun,
But unless you can handle endless hours, brother man,
If your lady invites you to come along
Just say 'I love you, but I've got to run!"

A Funny Story: My Uncle's Rebounding Hat

My Uncle Ted told me this story during a chat.
He called it the story of his rebounding hat;
Seems this incident occurred when he was nineteen
And used to pride himself in dressing up -- he called it "being mighty clean."
He was told by his older brother that,
While Ted was away at school, the church had come up with
a new entry rule,
That before he could enter the church,
A young man like him had to throw in his hat,
And if the hat was not thrown back at him
It was a sign that he could go right in.
Now, Uncle Ted felt that this was a funny rule
But, like I said, he always wanted to "play it cool."
So after driving over to church dressed in his sharp "Sunday go to meeting,"
He decided to follow his brother's advice
About this new manner of church greeting.
So after being greeted at the door by that Sunday's greeter "Brother Matt"
Uncle Ted promptly, obediently, removed his hat.
Now, Brother Matt expected that Ted would, of course, remove his hat,
But he was very shocked when Ted up and threw his hat.
He and Uncle Ted were even more surprised when Ted's hat
came flying back.
Then they heard a hearty laugh from the other side of the door.
Ted's brother, "Junior," was laughing so hard he was almost falling
to the floor.
Seems my uncle's brother had planned the whole thing as a joke.
And my uncle told me, if he had not been going into the church,
He would have hauled off and given his "jokester" brother
A well-deserved and hearty poke.

How I Got Over: That Ol' Bully

An Excerpt from My Childhood

When I was a little guy,
I had a mean 'ol cousin
Who consistently threatened to punch me in the eye.
Now, he was the age of twelve
And I was only seven,
But I knew that if he kept on being a bully,
That boy was never gonna get to no Heaven.
That overweight, ugly ol' rascal
Enjoyed bullying and chasing me; he was mean like that.
And sometimes he would threaten to
"knock my head clean off,"
Grinning that toothy grin while holding his baseball bat.
Like I said, he was way overweight
And a mean & right ornery pre-teen cuss
Who would say things like
"I'm gonna put a whoopin' on you" if I told on him,
Or if I put up a fuss.
Every time my mom and I would travel from the city
Out to my aunt and uncle's country farm,
That ol' rascal "Junior" would threaten to do me harm.
Well, I was taught in Sunday school
That the Good Lord will provide.
And when I recall how I got the best of that bully,
To this day I swell up with pride.
Well, one Saturday he was chasing me
And I had had just about enough.
So I turned around and put my hands on my hips
And decided to call his bluff.

I crossed my arms and said, "I see why you don't have a friend,
'cause you are mean and evil
And this bullying mess must come to an immediate end."
Would you believe that that big ol' rascal
Was so shocked that he started to cry.
Turned out that confronting him this way
Was more effective than a punch in the eye.
Well, seems like a hundred years have gone by
Since I escaped what could have been a disaster.
And would you also believe that my former bully cousin
Is now a very successful pastor!

My Hilarious Buddy -- Little Willie Smith

Here are some recollections from "way back when."
I want to share this with you,
but hardly know where to begin.
You, dear reader, might have heard or read my funny story about
Little Willie Smith, the only dude in our city neighborhood "who couldn't dance a lick."
Let me reiterate for those who have not heard or read me…
My teen pal, Little Willie Smith, who was all of five-foot three,
liked to use his paper route money to dress up for all to see,
And used to jump around like he was dancing
And, man, was that fun-ny!
But the funniest thing was on Saturdays when Willie would tag along to our favorite dance hall
And announce to anyone who would listen
"Tonight, your boy, Little Willie, is going to have himself a ball!"
Now, since Willie was my friend,
His character I will not besmirch.
But Willie would up and dance so weird,
That even the next day, Sunday,
we teens would still be thinking about him
and would sometimes find ourselves, despite ourselves,
smiling and laughing even during church.

Shopping: The Difference Between Women and Men

I've noticed that *sisters* of every age sure love to shop.
I believe that it's an instinct that starts at a *sister's* birth,
And isn't about to ever stop!
Now, I'm not knocking this activity that women love to do.
I'm just wonderin' why we men don't love to do it, too.

Oh, you say we men love to shop for some things, too,
But, Sisters, I have never known men who shop like you.
Sure, we like to shop for things like a brand-new car,
Just as long as the dealer is amenable to deal,
And his showroom is not too far.

But when men go looking for some raiment to wear,
We generally don't look at everything that they have in there,
Nor do we try on garment after garment, not able to choose among them.
Usually, we men get in and out of the store with one quickly selected item,

While my *Sisters*, loveable darlings that you are,
Are not about to select any garment in a measly hour.
It just might not feel right unless you shop till you drop,
And only physical or financial exhaustion is going to make you stop.

But I guess this divergence is put best by the French,
Who say about men and women, "Vive la différence!"

The Racist I Met One Day

One day, just before Christmas, I was in a famous clothing store.
Apparently, everybody was in a hurry to buy a little more,
As the store was very crowded due to its "holiday sale."
But instead of "Good Will to All," I met a racist
Motivating me to share with you this tale.
I was just about to get in line when this "cracker" pushed in front of me
Saying "Boy, get out of my way. I'm in a hurry, can't you see?"
Now, I consider myself a Christian, with love for all mankind.
But, I must admit that his arrogant disrespect was motivating me to up
and kick his rude behind.
I said "Sir, you are being rude and your conduct is appalling.
There was a time I would have followed my basic instincts
And right now you would be falling."
He got all red in the face and said, "You better hold your temper, boy.
Otherwise seeing you go to jail for assault would be my happy joy."
Well, at that point I did come close to losing my cool.
But, the Good Lord guided me to hold on, and not go "upside the head"
of "that fool."
Just then, a funny thing happened.
A "Sister" who had observed the whole incident,
Came up and pushed him forcefully out her way.
She said to him, "Fool, if you mess with me, I'll stomp you in the ground!"
Next thing I knew that mean ol' dude
Got out of the way and was suddenly nowhere to be found.

Sometimes You Have to Laugh

I have learned from experience and from incidents in my past
That sometimes you just need to "crack a smile" and
Sometimes you just need to laugh!
"What am I talking about?"
You are asking. Well, read on my friend
And you will plainly see.

If I see someone dancing
Who "can't dance a lick,"
I am not going to embarrass him,
But I'm going to laugh to myself real quick!

If I see a young teen man
Thinking he is "in style" with his pants falling down,
I'm not going to laugh in his face,
But I will cover my mouth
As I laugh at "the clown."

If I see a young teen lady
With way too much makeup
And looking like she's about to go "on stage,"
I'm not going to laugh at the young miss,
But I am going to be amused, I'm afraid.

If I see an aging brother
Acting like he's still a teen,
I'm not going to laugh in his face.
But later, I'm going to laugh
And scream!

If I go to a party
And see someone who is usually "uptight"
Get "high" and "act a fool,"
I'm not going to laugh in his face,
But I am going to laugh while I'm playing it "cool."

So, do you see what I mean
When I say sometimes you just have to laugh?
Well, everything I've cited here
Are actual incidents from my past.

Little Delights!

I MUST BE SUGAR

I must be sugar
Or something sweeter;
But, I'm mad as Hell
At this damn mosquito!

FINGER LICKIN'

Talk about something
That was Finger Lickin' --
There has never been a gourmet *anything*
Like my Mom's fried chicken.

NO NEED TO FROWN

Why do some folks walk around
With an ugly ol' frown
When they learn that their frown can be converted
Into a lovely smile,
If only turned upside down?

"HE" WILL PROSPER US

We Christian folk don't let the economy "bug" us,
'Cause the "God Lord" has promised
That, *through our Faith,*
He will prosper us!

BIOGRAPICAL SKETCH OF JAMES H. "DOC" LOCKHART, JR., Ed.D.

James H. "Doc" Lockhart, Jr., Ed.D., a resident of Rockville, Maryland, is a professional educator, nationally-known public speaker, award-winning poet, honored playwright and essayist, published author, community leader and church official. Dr. Lockhart has taught at the high school level (Albany and Schenectady (New York) public schools), and at the State University of New York at Albany. He served as a Program Specialist at the New York State Department of Education, and has worked with the U.S. Department of Education, monitoring educational programs, providing technical assistance to both officials and practitioners, and presenting at numerous conferences at the local, state and national levels.

Dr. Lockhart is excited to bring forth his latest poetic work, *"A Treasure Chest of the Best-Loved Poems of J.H. Lockhart."*

www.ingramcontent.com/pod-product-compliance
Lightning Source LLC
Chambersburg PA
CBHW020126130526
44591CB00032B/547